Starch

A Monologue

Geoff Saunders

A Samuel French Acting Edition

SAMUELFRENCH-LONDON.CO.UK
SAMUELFRENCH.COM

Copyright © 2006 by Geoff Saunders
All Rights Reserved

STARCH is fully protected under the copyright laws of the British Commonwealth, including Canada, the United States of America, and all other countries of the Copyright Union. All rights, including professional and amateur stage productions, recitation, lecturing, public reading, motion picture, radio broadcasting, television and the rights of translation into foreign languages are strictly reserved.

ISBN 978-0-573-14203-1

www.samuelfrench-london.co.uk

www.samuelfrench.com

For Amateur Production Enquiries

United Kingdom and World excluding North America

plays@SamuelFrench-London.co.uk

020 7255 4302/01

Each title is subject to availability from Samuel French,

depending upon country of performance.

CAUTION: Professional and amateur producers are hereby warned that *STARCH* is subject to a licensing fee. Publication of this play does not imply availability for performance. Both amateurs and professionals considering a production are strongly advised to apply to the appropriate agent before starting rehearsals, advertising, or booking a theatre. A licensing fee must be paid whether the title is presented for charity or gain and whether or not admission is charged.

The professional rights in this play are controlled by Samuel French Ltd, 52 Fitzroy Street, London, W1T 5JR.

No one shall make any changes in this title for the purpose of production. No part of this book may be reproduced, stored in a retrieval system, or transmitted in any form, by any means, now known or yet to be invented, including mechanical, electronic, photocopying, recording, videotaping, or otherwise, without the prior written permission of the publisher. No one shall upload this title, or part of this title, to any social media websites.

The right of Geoff Saunders to be identified as author of this work has been asserted by him in accordance with Section 77 of the Copyright, Designs and Patents Act 1988

STARCH

First presented in the kitchen of John and Sue March in Maltravers Street, Arundel on 20th August 2006, as part of the Arundel Festival Theatre Trail, with the following cast:

Charles John Griffiths

Directed by Bill Brennan

To
Martyn and Penny Andrews
with love and thanks

Also by Geoff Saunders published by Samuel French

Other People

STARCH

An ironing board with a plugged-in, practical iron on it. A small table with a bottle of spray starch and a jug of water on it. A clotheshorse with several empty coathangers on it. A chair with a pile of unironed shirts — all white — on it

The Lights come up on Charles, a well-spoken man in his mid-forties, halfway through ironing the first shirt. As the play proceeds he irons as many shirts as time allows and hangs each one on the clotheshorse. He is very careful about starching the collars and cuffs

Charles "Mr Thorogood, do you think this may have been a cry for help?" This, to me, from one of the policemen. Can't be more than twelve, by the looks of him; not convinced his voice has fully broken. I don't turn to face him, I just say "No, you fool, attempting suicide is a 'cry for help'; stealing a box of spark plugs and two batteries from Halfords hardly counts, does it?" I forbear to comment that attempted suicide is, in my book, a particularly stupid way to draw attention to oneself; who's to say one won't do the job properly by accident? No help to anybody.

Not planned, my first brush with major crime. I'm at the checkout, spark plugs and batteries in hand. Suddenly realize I've left my wallet at home. First thought is: put the stuff back on the shelf, go home, pick up the wallet, come back — but my second thought's kicked in by then, running something like this: "Just take them, Charles! Boy's faffing about behind the counter" — is this country run entirely by pre-pubescent bunglers, I wonder? —

"and I could so easily just walk out the door." So I do. Out the door with the spark plugs under my arm and the batteries in my hand with the car keys. Calm as you like, unbelievable — no excitement, no guilt, not even a sense of triumph, nothing. I just think "You've done it, mate. That'll serve 'em right for having such lousy security."

Tap on my shoulder at that point. Swing round and there, miles beneath me, it seems, is the boy from Halfords. Thin; pimply; glasses; braces on his teeth: the full regalia of the no-hope going-nowhere type. Sort of lad I'd have enjoyed baiting at school, given half the chance. Head Boy, couldn't really, but would have done. "How are you going to deal with this, then, sonny?" I think to myself.

"Excuse me, sir, I think you forgot to pay for your purchases," Pimple Boy squeaks. Another unbroken voice claiming authority over me. The wording, "I think you forgot," that annoys me. Guess the idea is it's quite possible to forget to pay and they shouldn't accuse you on the spot. Benefit of the doubt and all that. But, bugger it, I don't want any of that, do I? I've stolen the stuff — nicked it — and I want to be treated like a proper criminal. Not sure why, really. So I bark at Pimple Boy, "I didn't forget." "I'm sorry, sir, but you did," he replies, still not accusing me. "I didn't forget to pay," I repeat, leaning over to make my point and seeing myself reflected in his specs, which makes me feel even more of a crook. I'm enjoying myself now. "I didn't forget, because I never intended to pay. I stole these items." "In that case, sir, would you please accompany me back to the shop. We always prosecute shoplifters, so I am going to have to call the police." I don't put up a struggle; not a violent bloke. I let myself be led back to the shop. Twenty minutes later, cop car turns up and off we go. Get to the station and the Metropolitan Police's teenage Sigmund Freud starts his psychological dissection.

"Have you ever shoplifted before, Mr Thorogood?" he asks me. Answer's no, of course. I don't mention getting as far as the door of Woolworth's with a bag of Pick 'n' Mix, age nine, and then turning back. Then Sigmund deviates from the sort of questioning I'd expect, says uncharacteristic behaviour like this often stems from personal trauma: have I experienced anything traumatic recently? Tell him, "Of course not, " obviously. Not until I'm on the way home that it occurs to me: perhaps Jean leaving me for Malcolm Bentley could be seen as a "personal trauma". Must admit, though, that even if I'd thought of that when he asked me, I wouldn't have mentioned it. What's it got to do with him?

Never gone in much for this idea that one event in your life can influence another. Jean does it all the time; she'll have a blow-up about something, then say "Sorry I got so angry; it wasn't you, really, it was just that the situation reminded me of that big row I had with my mother in 1964," as if that excuses the broken crockery and embarrassed dinner guests. Everything's excusable in that philosophy; not sure I'm happy about that. Gay men, too; we've had several at Parker and Thompson over the years — Marketing Department, naturally — and they're all adept at finding these little connections between past and present. Get women and gay men together raking through their psychological wreckage and they're unstoppable.

Get them on to any subject and they're the same, really. Talk talk talk.

Guess that's why I thought Howard Baxter was gay. Sales, not Marketing, but nevertheless. Naomi Jarrett asks him one morning, "How are you, Howard?" He doesn't just say "Fine" as I would, he actually tells her. Health, state of mind, plans for the weekend, what he's seen on TV the night before, everything. Can't say I've ever heard a man talk like that before. Really quite bizarre.

Another clue to his sexuality, I thought, incidentally: his clothes. Every day, for all the twenty years I've been at Parker and Thompson, I've worn a charcoal grey suit and a white shirt, letting my tie alone provide a splash of colour and personality. Howard Baxter swans in on his first day in a flashy designer suit with a yellow shirt and an extremely lurid tie. It's as if he's saying "Me, I'm all personality." He just has to be gay. Turns out, of course, he's nothing of the sort, he's just young, and confident and articulate — and, it has to be said, he has the pick of the girls.

Made the same mistake over Malcolm Bentley, actually. Never imagined my marriage was in any danger from that quarter. Antiques dealer, for starters. Jean collects Wedgwood, doesn't she; can't stand it myself, can't use it after all and what's the point of having things just to look at? Damn stuff has to be valued for the insurance, so Polly bloody Marchwood — fine friend she turned out to be — recommends Malcolm, Jean calls him up and over he comes. Have him summed up in an instant. Tight trousers, moustache, pastel jumper over his shoulders, sunglasses on a chain round his neck — I ask you — and he never stops bloody talking. Greets Jean with compliments about her appearance — can't remember what she was wearing, probably nothing special — and minces around the house going "Oh, that's wonderful," and "That's quite, quite exquisite," as she points out her favourite figurines and rose bowls and bloody Ming bloody vases or whatever they are, don't know, don't care. Having whipped him up into a fever of antique-lover's lust she takes him into the back dining-room, which she, with characteristic pretension, calls "The Wedgwood Room" and he virtually explodes on the spot. He launches into another "Oh, exquisite, delightful, gorgeous" monologue — more like an operatic aria, now I come to think of it — so I beat a hasty retreat. Nauseating though he is, it never occurs to me to question or disapprove of the repeated visits he makes over the coming months; I never suspect they're for anything but girly tea-parties with his new chum Jean. As long as I don't have to spend any time with him myself, I don't give a damn. And Jean never makes excuses; if I say "What have you been up to today, poppet?" she'll say, "Oh, Malcolm came round this afternoon," not bothering to add "He wanted another look at the Wedgwood," or anything like that. And what do I do? I tell her: "It's so good you've found a friend, Jean."

Few weeks later, the long arm of irony smacks me in the face good and proper. She tells me she's leaving me for Malcolm Bentley. Chucks a lot of stuff at me, then moves in for the *coup de grâce*. "You know the best thing about Malcolm, dear?" I'm wincing already, dreading a report on their athletic lovemaking or some such, but she says, "I can talk to Malcolm. Really talk. And he really talks to me. We communicate, Charles. Something you and I have never done." "That's because I never get a bloody word in edgeways," I bellow at her, somewhat unfairly, I admit, but she ignores me anyway. "You're just so boring, Charles," she says. "I could never chat with you, could I? And I can with Malcolm, so I'm going to live with him." Not quite as blunt as that, obviously, but that's the gist.

Later on, of course, I have to ask her about the sex. Don't really want to know, but at the same time I do. "Who's better then, Jean?" I ask her, "Malcolm or me?" "It isn't a case of one of you being better, " she replies. "It's just — different with him." And she goes on again about preferring him because he can chat. Chat. Seems she'd rather have a little chin-wag with old Malcolm than a damn good bed session with me. Puts me in my place and no mistake.

Never been a chatter myself, really. Can't see the point of it. I'm a headline man. Dad was the same. You fall over and scrape your knee at school. Dad says: "Are you dead?" "No." Are you badly injured?" "No." Do I need to drive you anywhere or pay money to anyone?" "No." "Good. Run along." The bare facts are all he needs, see?

Lots of my school mates came from really "hip" families, some of them aristocratic dropouts with tons of inherited money, some weekend hippies with jobs in the city, all of them rich enough to have time and leisure to sit about for hours plotting the death of Capitalism. My mate Edmond can be found of an evening smoking home-grown pot with his father, listening to Lou Reed and discussing sex, politics, revolution — and, age sixteen, I'm envious. Not of the pot or the Lou Reed, really — pot makes me feel sick and I'm more of a Shadows fan — but envious of the conversation. Edmond and his dad really know each other, or seem to, and I suddenly get it into my head that I should make an attempt to communicate with mine, break down the barriers of stuffy English convention that oppress us both. Not convinced it's a good idea, not convinced this sort of thing's really in my nature, but anyway — I take my courage in my hands and raid his study.

He's in his big high-backed leather armchair reading the *Telegraph*. Beethoven sonatas on the gramophone. Pipe burning. He looks up at me as if I'm the most disgusting sight he's ever seen and says, "You didn't knock, Charles." God knows where my nerve comes from; I reply "No, I didn't. It's that sort of formality that puts fences between people and now's the time to break them down." "Oh, really," he says. "Yeah," I reply, and he grimaces. He hates slackness of speech and particularly loathes Americanisms. I take a deep breath and trot out my prepared speech: "Dad, I need, your help. It's about girls." "Girls?" he asks. "And why do you need advice from me on that subject?" "Because everyone at school goes on and on about kissing them and having sex with them, Dad, and I can't even talk to a girl without feeling really embarrassed and stupid ..." He holds up his hand. "That's quite enough," he says. "Talk to the Chaplain at school; that's what he's there for." "But all my friends talk to their fathers about this stuff, Dad; I thought I should talk to you." "I see. And do your friends' fathers give them advice?" "Yes, Dad." "And do they follow the advice?"

Good point. I don't tell Dad that even my mates with "hip" fathers don't take the blindest bit of notice of what they tell them. In fact, as far as I can see the way to respond to a father's advice is to do exactly the opposite of what he suggests. You ask for advice in order to have something to react to; that's the system.

I'm silent too long. Dad says, "I'm not giving advice that's not going to be acted upon." Guessing exactly what has been going through my head. "If you can't talk to the Chaplain about it — and I don't blame you, son, after all, what the hell's he going to know about it — then talk to your mother." And our interview's over. It — and the subject — never mentioned again. Never make another attempt. Not in my nature, breaking down fences. Keep them up, I reckon. They're there for a reason, after all.

And there's no way I'm going to talk to Mum, is there? The embarrassment. Mum wouldn't have wanted to know, anyway. Those days, women didn't want to see your weaknesses; they needed to believe their men were invincible. All different now; it's a given nowadays that men are pathetic and useless. The press and TV are full of man-baiting; all the ills of the world are caused by men, women can do perfectly well without them, men are shown up as stupid and clumsy and — oh bloody dear — unemotional and are more or less redundant.

Dad would have hated this "brave new world" — good job he died when he did.

Mum's sitting on a bench in the graveyard having a bit of a weep, fair enough, and she says "You know, Charles, your father never said he loved me, even when we were courting. It just wasn't his way, was it?" Jean is horrified — she comes from one of those families where they're forever flinging their arms around each other — and she says "Charles, you've never told me you love me either. You're just like your father." She makes me promise to tell her I love her at least once a day in case — can't believe she says this — in case one of us should die in the night. So I do. Every bloody day. Very embarrassing.

Mum was right, though, about Dad. He never said anything nice, you'd have to ... what's the word ... sort of — decode it from the few words he did say. He looks at your school report and says, "Your Geography's improving, Charles," and you know that means "I'm proud of you, son," and that's all you need. God forbid he should actually tell you he's proud of you or anything like that — you wouldn't know where to put yourself.

"You're just like your father. You're just like your father."

He irons for a while, thoughtfully. Then he stops ironing

Here's a new thought. Never made the connection before. Jean's right. It's not just coincidence that we're similar; his nature explains mine. He never gave anything away, I never give anything away, can't see the point. And it's that that's brought about my downfall with Jean — or given her a damn good excuse, anyway.

He starts ironing again

Going to lose my bloody job, I've no doubt. Didn't want to make a "diminished responsibility" plea to the court, want my punishment fair and square, so I can hardly ask Parker and Thompson for sympathy, can I? Shan't blame 'em if they do give me the elbow — after all, a Head of Accounts who's not completely squeaky-clean hardly gives you confidence. Still, they can't fault me for not being up-front about my misdemeanour. Into old Parker's office first thing, told him all. Better that than he read it in the local rag and wonder why I'd covered it up. He's behind his desk, checking some figures. Does his trademark trick; doesn't look up for ages, keeps me standing in front of him like a bloody naughty schoolboy. Light gleaming off his shiny bald pate and Himmler specs. The old git. Tell him my story. Takes it all in total silence, then says "We'll have to have a board meeting about this, Thorogood." No "Charles, old boy" for me that morning. "I shall check your work every day," he tells me, "and the banking will be counted twice in my presence or that of Mr Thompson. That is all."

"That is all."

He stops ironing

So, I'm just like my father, am I? But no-one ever treated him like a fool. Everyone respected him. I respected him, in my own way. But has anyone — anyone — ever respected me? Like hell they have. The bastards.

Never talked like this before. Never joined the dots up and tried to make sense of things. Never needed to. But now it all falls into place.

I don't have to let the bastards squash the life out of me, do I? Why give them the satisfaction? That copper was right. Nicked that stuff from Halfords for a reason. Need to be different, shake myself up a bit. Why not — my God, am I really thinking like this?— why not cut loose, make a fresh start? I could hand in my notice Monday morning. No wife, no job, respectable savings, divorce won't cost a bomb, fine for the shoplifting won't be much ... Yes, it's simple! I can do it! Monday morning — give Parker and Thompson the old heave-ho. Monday afternoon — put this house on the market; why not? Then chuck a brick through Malcolm Bentley's window and it's off into the sunset. No more conservative Charles — clap hands, here comes Charlie!

Then again, perhaps I should wait and see — maybe they won't sack me. Don't want to be too hasty ...

No, Charlie, don't go back. No doubts, no indecisions. If you don't change, you'll go under, and (*in his father's voice*) "a Thorogood never goes under". Don't wait till Monday, get the ball rolling right now — phone that old bastard Parker and tell him you're off!

He takes the white shirt from the ironing board and screws it up during the following

> Mr Parker, darling Jean, bloody Malcolm Bentley; Sigmund Freud, Pimple Boy, the whole damn lot of you ——

He puts the crumpled shirt on the ironing board and presses the iron down hard on it

> That is all.

He puts the crumpled shirt on a hanger and places it in line with the others

> *He exits*

BLACK-OUT

FURNITURE AND PROPERTY LIST

On stage: Ironing board. *On it*: practical iron
Small table. *On it*: bottle of spray starch, jug of water
Clotheshorse. *On it*: several empty clotheshangers
Chair. *On it*: pile of unironed, white shirts

LIGHTING PLOT

Property fittings required: nil
Interior. The same scene throughout

To open: General interior lighting

Cue 1   **Charles** exits (Page 10)
          Black-out

EFFECTS PLOT

No cues

Printed by The Kingfisher Press, London NW10 7AS

www.ingramcontent.com/pod-product-compliance
Lightning Source LLC
Chambersburg PA
CBHW070456050426
42450CB00012B/3303